CATS

A PORTRAIT IN PICTURES AND WORDS

CATS

A PORTRAIT IN PICTURES AND WORDS

CHARLOTTE FRASER

A HERMAN GRAF BOOK
SKYHORSE PUBLISHING

Copyright © Summersdale Publishers, 2013
First North American edition by Skyhorse Publishing, 2014
Photographs © Shutterstock
Published by arrangement with Summersdale Publishers Ltd.

Skyhorse Publishing books may be purchased in bulk at special discounts for sales promotion, corporate gifts, fund-raising, or educational purposes. Special editions can also be created to specifications. For details, contact the Special Sales Department, Skyhorse Publishing, 307 West 36th Street, 11th Floor, New York, NY 10018 or info@skyhorsepublishing.com.

Skyhorse® and Skyhorse Publishing® are registered trademarks of Skyhorse Publishing, Inc.®, a Delaware corporation.

Visit our website at www.skyhorsepublishing.com.

10 9 8 7 6 5 4 3 2 1

Library of Congress Cataloging-in-Publication Data is available on file.

Cover image credit Shutterstock

ISBN: 978-1-62914-772-7
E-book ISBN: 978-1-62914-900-4

Printed in China

INTRODUCTION

Cats were first domesticated an estimated 10,000 years ago in the Middle East. Since then, felines have been worshipped and loved by humans, from Ancient Egyptian times to the present day, aesthetically for their image of perfection, grace and poise, or simply for their calming presence and companionship.

Known as majestic and mysterious creatures, their beguiling presence has inspired some of the most renowned writers, painters, psychologists and celebrities alike. T. S. Eliot, Pablo Picasso and Sigmund Freud are among those who have contributed to the portrayal and analysis of the feline's impenetrable, yet compelling, demeanour, in one way or another, highlighting the significant impact they have on our lives. Even as far back as the fifteenth century, evidence shows that one writer and his cat were literally inseparable, when a number of inky prints marked by the cat's paws were discovered in the pages of a medieval Italian manuscript.

As cats have become part of our homes and families over the centuries, they have also grown into one of our greatest comforts and joys. Jean Cocteau's knowing comment, 'I love cats because I enjoy my home; and little by little, they become its visible soul', is an underlying truth for anyone who has ever owned a cat.

To celebrate the feline in all its forms and beauty, and to mark our timeless affection for this transcendental animal, this collection of stunning photographs and elegant prose, poetry and quotes offers a full spectrum of our wonderful friend, the cat.

He lives in the halflights in secret places, free and alone – this mysterious little great being…

MARGARET BENSON

See the Kitten on the wall,
Sporting with the leaves that fall,
Withered leaves – one – two – and three –
From the lofty elder-tree!
Through the calm and frosty air
Of this morning bright and fair,
Eddying round and round they sink
Softly, slowly: one might think,
From the motions that are made,
Every little leaf conveyed
Sylph or Faery hither tending,
To this lower world descending,
Each invisible and mute,
In his wavering parachute.
– But the Kitten, how she starts,
Crouches, stretches, paws, and darts!
First at one, and then its fellow
Just as light and just as yellow;
There are many now – now one –
Now they stop and there are none:
What intenseness of desire
In her upward eye of fire!

WILLIAM WORDSWORTH, FROM 'THE KITTEN AND THE FALLING LEAVES'

*There is no more
intrepid explorer than a kitten.*

JULES CHAMPFLEURY

A cat will do what it wants when it wants,
and there's not a thing you can do about it.

FRANK PERKINS

Lat take a cat, and fostre hym wel with milk,
And tendre flessh, and make his couche of silk,
And lat hym seen a mous go by the wal,
Anon he weyveth milk and flessh and al,
And every deyntee that is in that hous,
Swich appetit he hath to ete a mous.
Lo, heere hath lust his dominacioun,
And appetit fleemeth discrecioun.

GEOFFREY CHAUCER, *THE CANTERBURY TALES*

The cat does not offer services.
The cat offers itself.

WILLIAM S. BURROUGHS

There is a cat I see in the corner – a pretty cat – look at her – observe her well. Now, Bon-Bon, do you behold the thoughts – the thoughts, I say, – the ideas – the reflections – which are being engendered in her pericranium? There it is, now – you do not! She is thinking we admire the length of her tail and the profundity of her mind. She has just concluded that I am the most distinguished of ecclesiastics, and that you are the most superficial of metaphysicians.

EDGAR ALLAN POE, 'WHY THE LITTLE FRENCHMAN WEARS HIS HAND IN A SLING'

The smallest feline is a masterpiece.

LEONARDO DA VINCI

A cat is there when you call her – if she doesn't have something better to do.

BILL ADLER

... a cat is only
      technically an animal,
            being divine.

ROBERT LYND

There are few things in life more heartwarming than to be welcomed by a cat.

TAY HOHOFF

Over the hearth with my 'minishing eyes I muse; until after
the last coal dies.
Every tunnel of the mouse,
every channel of the cricket,
I have smelt,
I have felt
the secret shifting of the mouldered rafter,
and heard
every bird in the thicket.
I see
you
Nightingale up in the tree!
I, born of a race of strange things,
of deserts, great temples, great kings,
in the hot sands where the nightingale never sings!

FORD MADOX FORD, 'THE CAT OF THE HOUSE'

Minnaloushe runs in the grass,
Lifting his delicate feet.
Do you dance, Minnaloushe, do you dance?
When two close kindred meet
What better than call a dance?
Maybe the moon may learn,
Tired of that courtly fashion,
A new dance turn.

Minnaloushe creeps through the grass
From moonlit place to place,
The sacred moon overhead
Has taken a new phase.
Does Minnaloushe know that his pupils
Will pass from change to change,
And that from round to crescent,
From crescent to round they range?

Minnaloushe creeps through the grass
Alone, important and wise,
And lifts to the changing moon
His changing eyes.

W. B. YEATS, FROM 'THE CAT AND THE MOON'

Her coat was made up of patches of yellow and white, varied with a black stocking on her right hind leg, and a large, round, black spot about her right eye, which gave her a peculiarly predatory and disreputable appearance... There was something demoniac in her cleverness, her immunity from harm, her prodigious energy, her malevolent mischief, her raillery.

CHARLES MINER THOMPSON, *THE CALICO CAT*

Dear creature by the fire a-purr,
Strange idol, eminently bland,
Miraculous puss! As o'er your fur
I trail a negligible hand,
And gaze into your gazing eyes,
And wonder in a demi-dream,
What mystery it is that lies,
Behind those slits that glare and gleam,
An exquisite enchantment falls
About the portals of my sense;
Meandering through enormous halls,
I breathe luxurious frankincense…

LYTTON STRACHEY, FROM 'THE CAT'

*Which is more beautiful
– feline movement or feline stillness?*

ELIZABETH HAMILTON

*Friendship is a single soul
　　　　　dwelling in two bodies.*

ARISTOTLE

Like a graceful vase, a cat, even
when motionless, seems to flow.

GEORGE F. WILL

*A kitten is the most irresistible comedian
in the world. Its wide-open eyes
gleam with wonder and mirth.*

AGNES REPPLIER

For I will consider my Cat Jeoffry...
For in his morning orisons he loves the sun and the sun loves him.
For he is of the tribe of Tiger.
For the Cherub Cat is a term of the Angel Tiger.
For he has the subtlety and hissing of a serpent, which in
goodness he suppresses.
For he will not do destruction, if he is well-fed, neither will he
spit without provocation.
For he purrs in thankfulness, when God tells him he's a good Cat.

CHRISTOPHER SMART, FROM 'JUBILATE AGNO'

A little drowsing cat is
an image of perfect beatitude.

JULES CHAMPFLEURY

I believe cats to be spirits come to earth. A cat, I am sure, could walk on a cloud without coming through.

JULES VERNE

It's really the cat's house
       – we just pay the mortgage.

ANONYMOUS

A gentleman had a favourite cat whom he taught to sit at the dinner table where it behaved very well. He was in the habit of putting any scraps he left onto the cat's plate. One day puss did not take his place punctually, but presently appeared with two mice, one of which it placed on its master's plate, the other on its own.

BEATRIX POTTER, *BEATRIX POTTER'S JOURNAL*

*There are no grades of vanity, there are
only grades of ability in concealing it.*

MARK TWAIN

The dawn was apple-green,
The sky was green wine held up in the sun,
The moon was a golden petal between.

She opened her eyes, and green
They shone, clear like flowers undone
For the first time, now for the first time seen.

D. H. LAWRENCE, 'GREEN'

*Happy is the home
        with at least one cat.*

Cats always seem so very wise, when
staring with their half-closed eyes.

BETTE MIDLER

Prowling his own quiet backyard or asleep by the fire, he is still only a whisker away from the wilds.

JEAN BURDEN

In ancient times
cats were worshipped as gods;
they have not forgotten this.

TERRY PRATCHETT

In reverie they emulate the noble mood
Of giant sphinxes stretched in depths of solitude
Who seem to slumber in a never-ending dream;

Within their fertile loins a sparkling magic lies;
Finer than any sand are dusts of gold that gleam,
Vague starpoints, in the mystic iris of their eyes.

CHARLES BAUDELAIRE, FROM 'CATS'

The cat is nature's beauty.

FRENCH PROVERB

… the cat. He walked by himself,
and all places were alike to him.

RUDYARD KIPLING

When sorrows press my heart I say:
Maybe they'll disappear one day:
When books will be my friends at night,
My darling then: the candle light,
My sweetest friend: a kitten white!

AL-DAMIRI

*Everything a cat is and does physically
is to me beautiful, lovely, stimulating,
soothing, attractive and an enchantment.*

PAUL GALLICO

Arise from sleep, old cat,
and with great yawns
and stretchings…
Amble out for love

KOBAYASHI ISSA

There is something about the presence of a cat...
that seems to take the bite out of being alone.

LOUIS J. CAMUTI

How dull our World would be, and flat,
Without the Golden Pussy Cat.

OLIVER HERFORD, FROM 'THE GOLDEN CAT'

Freedom lies in being bold.

ROBERT FROST

The ideal of calm
          exists in a sitting cat.

If it's raining at the back door, every cat is convinced there's a good chance that it won't be raining at the front door.

WILLIAM TOMS

It is a very inconvenient habit of kittens (Alice had once made the remark) that, whatever you say to them, they always purr.

LEWIS CARROLL, *THROUGH THE LOOKING-GLASS*

Kittens large and Kittens small,
Prowling on the Back Yard Wall,
Though your fur be rough and few,
I should like to play with you.
Though you roam the dangerous street,
And have curious things to eat,
Though you sleep in barn or loft,
With no cushions warm and soft,
Though you have to stay out-doors
When it's cold or when it pours,
Though your fur is all askew—
How I'd like to play with you!

OLIVER HERFORD, 'FOREIGN KITTENS'

I was separated from my mother at a very early age, and sent out into the world alone, long before I had had time to learn to say 'please' and 'thank you,' and to shut the door after me, and little things like that. One of the things I had not learned to understand was the difference between milk in a saucer on the floor, and milk in a jug on the table. Other cats tell me there is a difference, but I can't see it. The difference is not in the taste of the milk – that is precisely the same.

E. NESBIT, *PUSSY AND DOGGY TALES*

Drowsing, they take the noble attitude
Of a great sphinx, who, in a desert land,
sleeps always, dreaming dreams
that have no end.

CHARLES BAUDELAIRE

*The cat is the only animal without
visible means of support who still
manages to find a living in the city.*

CARL VAN VECHTEN

Begin, be bold,
     and venture to be wise.

HORACE

Here to sit by me, and turn
Glorious eyes that smile and burn,
Golden eyes, love's lustrous meed,
On the golden page I read.

All your wondrous wealth of hair,
Dark and fair,
Silken-shaggy, soft and bright
As the clouds and beams of night,
Pays my reverent hand's caress
Back with friendlier gentleness.

ALGERNON CHARLES SWINBURNE, FROM 'TO A CAT'

In the other gardens
And all up the vale,
From the autumn bonfires
See the smoke trail!

Pleasant summer over
And all the summer flowers,
The red fire blazes,
The grey smoke towers.

Sing a song of seasons!
Something bright in all!
Flowers in the summer,
Fires in the fall!

ROBERT LOUIS STEVENSON, 'AUTUMN FIRES'

Long may you love your pensioner mouse,
Though one of a tribe that torment the house:
Nor dislike for her cruel sport the cat,
Deadly foe both of mouse and rat;
Remember she follows the law of her kind,
And Instinct is neither wayward nor blind.
Then think of her beautiful gliding form,
Her tread that would scarcely crush a worm,
And her soothing song by the winter fire,
Soft as the dying throb of the lyre.

DOROTHY WORDSWORTH, FROM 'LOVING AND LIKING'

Here we were at once attracted by the quantities of birds which flew from branch to branch above our heads, and twittered gaily in the fancied security of their leafy homes. We looked, and sniffed, and watched them as they flew, until our mouths watered at the sight. Having eaten nothing since morning, our appetites were very keen, and the thought of a little poultry was not by any means a disagreeable one… Although I knew perfectly well that it was a great sin, that the birds were not mine, and that I had not only no right to them, but no right either to be within those grounds, I was, in a moment of weakness, prevailed on to climb a lofty oak, and seize upon the contents of a nest we could discover among the branches.

ALFRED ELWES, *THE ADVENTURES OF A CAT*

It is a happy talent
to know how to play.

RALPH WALDO EMERSON

If there is one spot of sun spilling onto the floor, a cat will find it and soak it up.

J. A. MCINTOSH

The white saucer like some full moon descends
At last from the clouds of the table above;
She sighs and dreams and thrills and glows,
Transfigured with love.

She nestles over the shining rim,
Buries her chin in the creamy sea;
Her tail hangs loose; each drowsy paw
Is doubled under each bending knee.

A long, dim ecstasy holds her life;
Her world is an infinite shapeless white,
Till her tongue has curled the last holy drop,
Then she sinks back into the night,

Draws and dips her body to heap
Her sleepy nerves in the great arm-chair,
Lies defeated and buried deep
Three or four hours unconscious there.

HAROLD MONRO, FROM 'MILK FOR THE CAT'

Yes, there they were, big cats, very big cats,
middling-sized cats, and small cats,
cats of all colours and markings...

HARRISON WEIR

We need the tonic of wildness… At the same time that we are earnest to explore and learn all things, we require that all things be mysterious and unexplorable, that land and sea be indefinitely wild, unsurveyed and unfathomed by us because unfathomable. We can never have enough of nature.

HENRY DAVID THOREAU, *WALDEN: OR, LIFE IN THE WOODS*

I love cats because I enjoy my home; and little by little, they become its visible soul.

JEAN COCTEAU

Half loving-kindliness and half disdain,
Thou comest to my call serenely suave,
With humming speech and gracious gestures grave,
In salutation courtly and urbane;
Yet must I humble me thy grace to gain,
For wiles may win thee though no arts enslave,
And nowhere gladly thou abidest save
Where naught disturbs the concord of thy reign.
Sphinx of my quiet hearth! who deign'st to dwell
Friend of my toil, companion of mine ease
Thine is the lore of Ra and Rameses;
That men forget dost thou remember well,
Beholden still in blinking reveries
With sombre, sea-green gaze inscrutable.

ROSAMUND MARRIOTT WATSON, 'TO MY CAT'

The evening sun sinks low in the skies
The cat lies lazily blinking her eyes.
'Two little mice,
Some cream – so nice –
Four bits of fish
I stole from a dish;
I got all I desired,
And I'm lazy and tired,'
Says the cat.

BJORNSTJERNE BJORNSON, *A HAPPY BOY*

High up in the apple tree climbing I go,
With the sky above me, the earth below.
Each branch is the step of a wonderful stair
Which leads to the town I see shining up there.
Climbing, climbing, higher and higher,
The branches blow and I see a spire,
The gleam of a turret, the glint of a dome,
All sparkling and bright, like white sea foam.
On and on, from bough to bough,
The leaves are thick, but I push my way through;
Before, I have always had to stop,
But to-day I am sure I shall reach the top.
Today to the end of the marvellous stair,
Where those glittering pinnacles flash in the air!
Climbing, climbing, higher I go,
With the sky close above me, the earth far below.

AMY LOWELL, 'CLIMBING'

A wise parent humours the desire for independent action, so as to become the friend and advisor when his absolute rule shall cease.

ELIZABETH GASKELL, *NORTH AND SOUTH*

Cats are connoisseurs
of comfort.

JAMES HERRIOT

The cat, with eyes of burning coal,
Now Couches 'fore the mouse's hole.

WILLIAM SHAKESPEARE, *PERICLES, PRINCE OF TYRE*

The playful kitten, with its pretty little tigerish
gambols, is infinitely more amusing than half the
people one is obliged to live with in the world.

LADY SYDNEY MORGAN

One day last summer a large handsome black cat walked gravely up one side of Main Street, crossed, and went half-way down the other. He stopped at a house called The Den, went up the piazza steps, and paused by an open window.

A lady sitting inside saw and spoke to him; but without taking any notice, he put his paws on the sill, looked around the room as if wondering if it would suit him, and finally gazed into her face.

After thinking a minute he went in, and from that hour took his place as an important member of the family… No one at The Den can tell how he came to be called Plato. It is a fact that he answers to the name, and when asked if so known before he came there, smiles wisely. 'What matters it,' the smile says, 'how I was called, or where I came from, since I am Plato, and am here?'

A. S. DOWNS, *PLATO: THE STORY OF A CAT*

'Nature' is what we see –
The Hill – the Afternoon –
Squirrel – Eclipse – the Bumble bee –
Nay – Nature is Heaven –
Nature is what we hear –
The Bobolink – the Sea –
Thunder – the Cricket –
Nay – Nature is Harmony –
Nature is what we know –
Yet have no art to say –
So impotent Our Wisdom is
To her Simplicity.

EMILY DICKINSON, "NATURE" IS WHAT WE SEE'

A roof is not an ideal spot for bird study. I would hardly, out of preference, have chosen this with its soot and its battlement of gaseous chimney-pots... With the infinite number and variety of chimneys hedging me in, I naturally expected to find the sky alive with swallows. Indeed, I thought that some of the twenty-six pots at the corners of my roof would be inhabited by the birds. Not so.

DALLAS LORE SHARP, *ROOF AND MEADOW*

The cat is the animal to whom the Creator gave the biggest eye, the softest fur, the most supremely delicate nostrils, a mobile ear, an unrivalled paw and a curved claw borrowed from the rose-tree.

COLETTE

Kittens, you are very little,
And your kitten bones are brittle,
If you'd grow to Cats respected,
See your play be not neglected.

Smite the Sudden Spool, and spring
Upon the Swift Elusive String,
Thus you learn to catch the wary
Mister Mouse or Miss Canary.

OLIVER HERFORD, FROM 'GOOD AND BAD KITTENS'

The cats knew very well by this sign that breakfast was over; after the plate was set on that shelf, they never had a mouthful more of meat; and it was droll to see the change that came over all of them as soon as they saw this done. In less than a second, they changed from fierce, fighting, clawing, scratching, snatching, miaowing, spitting, growling cats, into quiet, peaceful cats, some sitting down licking their paws, or washing their faces, and some lying out full-length on the ground and rolling; some walking off in a leisurely and dignified manner, as if they had had all they wanted, and wouldn't thank anybody for another bit of meat, if they could have it as well as not.

HELEN HUNT JACKSON, *THE HUNTER CATS OF CONNORLOA*

Long ago, the mice had a general council to consider what measures they could take to outwit their common enemy, the Cat. Some said this, and some said that; but at last a young mouse got up and said he had a proposal to make, which he thought would meet the case. 'You will all agree,' said he, 'that our chief danger consists in the sly and treacherous manner in which the enemy approaches us. Now, if we could receive some signal of her approach, we could easily escape from her. I venture, therefore, to propose that a small bell be procured, and attached by a ribbon round the neck of the Cat. By this means we should always know when she was about, and could easily retire while she was in the neighbourhood.'

This proposal met with general applause, until an old mouse got up and said: 'That is all very well, but who is to bell the Cat?' The mice looked at one another and nobody spoke. Then the old mouse said:

'It is easy to propose impossible remedies.'

AESOP. *AESOP'S FABLES*

It seems that every glance she's ever met
She conceals somewhere deep inside,
The better to toy with it, to vex and threaten
With looking: and finally to sleep with it.
But one time she will turn, as if awakened, with
her face set squarely in the middle of yours:

And there you'll find your own gaze reflected
In the round and lovely stones of her amber eyes,
Unlooked for, too, and kept in that prison
Like some species of insect long gone from the earth.

RAINER MARIA RILKE, FROM 'BLACK CAT'

A murmur in the trees to note,
Not loud enough for Wind;
A Star not far enough to seek,
Nor near enough to find;

A long, long Yellow on the Lawn,
A Hubbub as of feet;
Not audible as ours to us,
But dapperer, more Sweet;

A hurrying home of little men
To houses unperceived,
All this, and more, if I should tell,
Would never be believed.

Of robins in the trundle bed
How many I espy
Whose nightgowns could not hide the wings,
Although I heard them try!

But then I promised ne'er to tell;
How could I break my word?
So go your way and I'll go mine,
No fear you'll miss the Road.

EMILY DICKINSON, 'A MURMUR IN THE TREES TO NOTE'

Cats are a mysterious kind of folk. There is more passing in their minds than we are aware of.

SIR WALTER SCOTT

The snow had begun in the gloaming,
And busily all the night
Had been heaping field and highway
With a silence deep and white.

Every pine and fir and hemlock
Wore ermine too dear for an earl,
And the poorest twig on the elm-tree
Was ridged inch deep with pearl.

JAMES RUSSELL LOWELL, FROM 'THE FIRST SNOW-FALL'

Our perfect companions never
have fewer than four feet.

COLETTE

Open your doors and take me in,
Spirit of the wood,
Wash me clean of dust and din,
Clothe me in your mood…

Lift your leafy roof for me,
Part your yielding walls;
Let me wander lingeringly
Through your scented halls.

Open your doors and take me in,
Spirit of the wood;
Take me – make me next of kin
To your leafy brood.

ETHELWYN WETHERALD, FROM 'THE HOUSE OF THE TREES'